NATIONAL WORLD WAR I MUSEUM
AT LIBERTY MEMORIAL

KANSAS CITY, MISSOURI

Copyright © 2009
National World War I Museum
at Liberty Memorial

National World War I Museum
at Liberty Memorial
100 W. 26th Street
Kansas City, Missouri 64108
(816) 784-1918
www.theworldwar.org

Content & Editing
Doran Cart, Jonathan Casey,
Eli Paul, Mary Shapiro, Carl
Strickwerda

Design & Art Direction
Tad Carpenter

Published by
Donning Company Publishers,
Marceline, MO

Project Managers
Kathy Jarboe, Eli Paul,
Denise Rendina

Front cover "Liberty Dusk &
Skyline," by Kevin Sink.

Photography
Eric Linebarger of
LemonLime Photography

Unless otherwise credited, all
photographs come from the
collections of the National
World War I Museum and
are available through its
Research Center.

Printed in the United States of
America at Walsworth Publishing
Company

Library of Congress Cataloging-in-Publication Data

Paul, R. Eli, 1954-
  National World War I Museum at Liberty Memorial / by R. Eli Paul.
    p. cm.
  ISBN 978-1-57864-569-5
  1. World War, 1914-1918–Exhibitions. 2. National World War I Museum at
Liberty Memorial–Exhibitions. I. Title.
  D503.P38 2009
  940.3074'778411–dc22
                                    2009017590

TABLE OF CONTENTS

Foreword	4
1914—1917	7
1917—1919	30
Liberty Memorial	56

FOREWORD

THE WORLD WAR, 1914-1919

At the beginning of the twentieth century a conflict in Europe rapidly escalated into a war of unprecedented destruction and bloodshed. About sixty-five million soldiers fought, and more than nine million died. The war involved thirty-six countries, including the United States, which sent two million men and women overseas. In the course of a few years, old empires fell, and the map of the world was redrawn. When the guns on the Western Front finally fell silent on November 11, 1918, peace—and an unstable one at that—did not officially come until the next year. Kansas City and this part of the nation took the lead to remember, memorialize, and learn the lessons from the war.

Just two weeks after the 1918 Armistice, Kansas Citians embarked on a campaign to create a memorial "in honor of those who served in the World War in defense of liberty and our country." A 1919 fund drive raised $2.5 million in two weeks. The enormous amount of money donated prompted a national architectural competition, which ultimately resulted in the architectural wonder that opened to the public in 1926. Subsequent world events—stock market collapse, economic depression and a second, "greater" world war—probably kept similar sized efforts to memorialize the service of those millions and to preserve their history from being undertaken, even in our nation's capital.

We are still taking the lead in remembering this "war to end all wars." The National World War I Museum at Liberty Memorial, officially designated by the 108th U.S. Congress in 2004, is the only American museum dedicated solely to preserving the materials, history, and personal experiences of the Great War. Dramatically expanded and opened to the public in 2006, the museum remains committed to sharing the stories of those who experienced this global, transformative event, the consequences of which are still with us.

We hope that this publication becomes one way to remember your visit and to recall the courage, honor, patriotism, and sacrifice of all who served in the World War.

Brian Alexander
President & Chief Executive Officer
National World War I Museum at Liberty Memorial

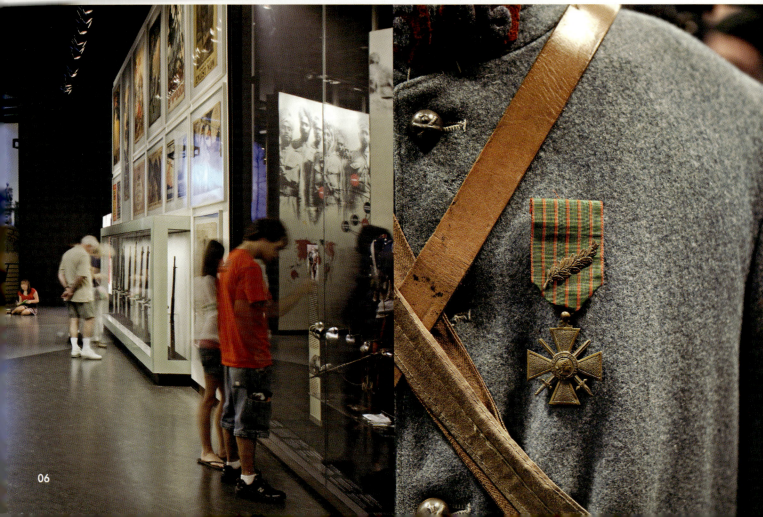

1914-1917

In 1914 Europe was at the height of its power, and pre-war London, as exemplified by Big Ben, was the financial capital of the world. A century of relative peace had brought great prosperity. Europeans had created a modern industrial society, and their empires controlled half of the world's surface and resources.

But beneath the economic and political success lay deep tensions. National rivalries lead to the formation of rigid military alliances and an unbridled arms race. Ethnic minorities struggled for their own national identities. Europe became divided into two rival coalitions: France, Great Britain, and Russia versus Germany, Austria-Hungary, and Italy (which later switched). Pistol shots in a Sarajevo street, whose bullets killed a head-of-state on June 28, 1914, served to push a world on the edge and led these countries to commence a devastating war.

Austria-Hungary's declaration of war on Serbia triggered a chain reaction of mobilizations and war declarations. Reservists put on old uniforms of red and blue, picked up their rifles, and boarded trains that would take them to the front. Both sides believed their cause was just, that they were defending their homelands and ways of life. Most imagined that the war would be a short, glorious affair, filled with colorful flags, flashing sabers, and heroic deeds. They thought they would all be home for Christmas.

1914: CALL TO ARMS

By August 4 the five Great Powers were at war. Russia, France, and Great Britain (the Allies) came to Serbia's aid against Germany and Austria-Hungary (the Central Powers). Germany, faced with a two-front war, set in motion its Schlieffen Plan, invading France through Belgium. It hoped to quickly capture Paris, then rush its troops to its eastern border to defeat Russia. But French and British forces stopped the Germans at the Marne River, north of Paris. Each army's attempt to outflank the other stalemated, forming the so-called Western Front—a four-hundred-mile stretch from the English Channel to the Swiss Alps. On the Eastern Front a vast Russian army took on a much smaller force of Germans and Austro-Hungarians, but by the year's end neither side had gained an advantage.

The Chronology Wall gives a month-by-month account of the war.

> "The lamps are going out all over Europe. We shall not see them lit again in our lifetime."

Edward, Viscount Grey of Falloden, British Foreign Office, August 3, 1914.

World War I was the first global war. The conflict spread rapidly from the Balkans to engulf all of Europe, which then mobilized its commonwealths and colonies around the world. Although Europe was the main battleground, fighting also took place in the Near East, Africa, China, and on the world's oceans. Before its conclusion, the warring nations would mobilize more than sixty-seven million men.

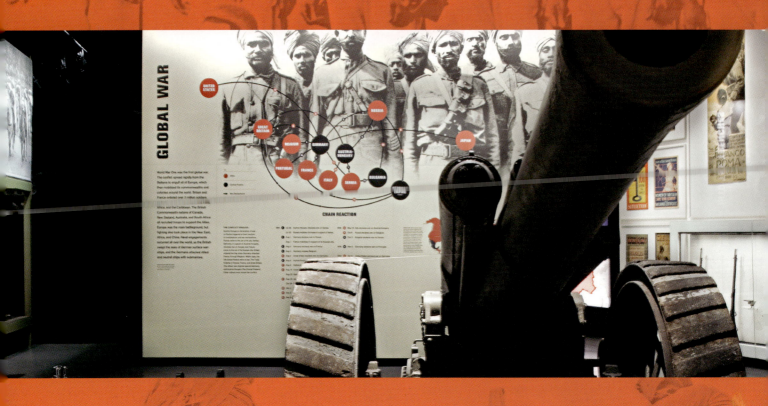

1914: CHAIN REACTION

JUL 28	Austria-Hungary declares war on Serbia.	**AUG 6**	Serbia declares war on Germany.
JUL 30	Russia mobilizes its troops in support of Serbia.	**AUG 12**	Great Britain declares war on Austria-Hungary.
AUG 1	France mobilizes in support of its Russian ally.	**AUG 23**	Japan declares war on Germany.
AUG 3	Germany declares war on France.	**OCT 29**	Turkey enters war on the German side.
AUG 3	Germany invades Belgium.	**NOV 2**	Russia declares war on Turkey.
AUG 4	Great Britain declares war on Germany.	**NOV 6**	Great Britain declares war on Turkey.
AUG 6	Austria-Hungary declares war on Russia.	**NOV 6**	France declares war on Turkey.

Prussian enlisted man's spiked helmet

1915: MOMENTUM SHIFTS TO THE EAST

The Schlieffen Plan had failed, forcing Germany to change its tactics. Over the next year Germany concentrated more on the Eastern Front and succeeded in pushing the Russians back into their own territory. Austro-Hungarian troops, with German support, finally managed to defeat the Serbians. Britain, too, looked for an alternative to the stalemate on the Western Front. It turned its sights on the strategic Dardanelles, controlled by Turkey, Germany's ally. In the Battle of Gallipoli, however, British Empire and French troops were soundly defeated by the Turks and forced to withdraw. This was also the year that a German submarine sunk the passenger ship, the *Lusitania*, causing worldwide outrage. In response Kaiser Wilhelm II reluctantly stopped the practice of sinking passenger ships without warning.

1916: DEADLOCK AND FURY

To break the deadlock on the Western Front, the Allies and the Central Powers engaged in two colossal and futile battles—the Battle of Verdun and the Battle of the Somme. After months of fighting, neither side gained an advantage, but the casualty toll was high—one million for each side. On the Eastern Front, Russian General Brusilov managed to destroy the Austro-Hungarian army, but in the process his own army was crushed by the Germans, who rushed troops from the Western Front to stop the Russian offensive. On the Italian front the Austro-Hungarians invaded the Trentino, only to be turned back decisively by the Italians, until German troops were rushed to the rescue.

If a soldier dared to look over the front edge of his trench, he would see a narrow strip of barren land separating him from his enemy. This was no-man's-land, a nightmarish wasteland created by constant bombardment of modern artillery and rapid firing of machine guns.

INTO THE

Nothing symbolizes World War One more than trench warfare. After the failure of the German offensive in 1914, the armies in northern France found themselves in a stalemate – unable to outflank or break through their opponents' lines. Both sides dug deep trenches to protect their positions. By the end of 1914, a network of trenches extended over 400 miles across Belgium and France. Over the next four years, the lines would hardly move. Infantry charges, the traditional tactic to take a position, could rarely overwhelm troops in a strongly fortified trench. Defenders, armed with modern weapons such as machine guns and rapid-fire artillery, could devastate attackers and keep any capture of frontline trenches from becoming a breakthrough.

Nothing symbolizes World War One more than trench warfare. After the failure of the German offensive in 1914, the armies in northern France found themselves in a stalemate – unable to outflank or break through their opponents' lines. Both sides dug deep trenches to protect their positions. By the end of 1914, a network of trenches extended over 400 miles across Belgium and France. Over the next four years, the lines would hardly move. Infantry charges, the traditional tactic to take a position, could rarely overwhelm troops in a strongly fortified trench. Defenders, armed with modern weapons such as machine guns and rapid-fire artillery, could devastate attackers and keep any capture of frontline trenches from becoming a breakthrough.

(Left) German trench armor hearkened to an earlier, obsolete age of knights on horseback, but the nature of trench war soon demanded personal protective covering.

(Right) Hand grenades, also called "hand bombs," came in a variety of shapes and destructive power.

> "The frontline soldier was only concerned with a hundred yards or so on either side of him and that in front of him."
>
> George Coppard, Royal West Surrey Regiment

NO MAN'S LAND

If a soldier dared to look over the front edge of his trench, he would see a narrow strip of barren land separating him from his enemy. This was no-man's-land, an ancient term that gained terrible new meaning during World War One. The constant bombardment of modern artillery and rapid firing of machine guns created a nightmarish wasteland, littered with tree stumps and snarls of barbed wire. In battle, soldiers had to charge across no-man's-land into a hail of bullets and shrapnel. They were easy targets, and casualties were enormously high. By the end of the war, total deaths exceeded all the deaths from all the wars for the previous hundred years.

MODERN WAR
World War One was the first conflict among industrialized nations. Countries at war mobilized their vast industrial resources to meet the soaring demands of the battlefield. Weapons producers dramatically increased their outputs. Factories that before the war had produced automobiles, steel for railways, and ships retooled to produce munitions, guns, and armor. More weapons meant more killing: casualties grew apace with increased arms production.

Nothing symbolizes World War I more than trench warfare. After the failure of the German offensive in 1914, the armies in northern France found themselves in a stalemate — unable to outflank or break through their opponents' lines — and dug in. By the end of 1914 a network extended over four hundred miles across Belgium and France, and almost four million soldiers faced each other in their trenches along the Western Front.

British Whitehead torpedo, Mark 1, made in the U.S. This type was used on British, French, Russian, and Japanese submarines.

The sinking of the *Lusitania* in 1915 served as inspiration for this American poster, one of the treasures of the museum collections.

WAR AT SEA

When war broke out, Great Britain used its larger navy to blockade German ports. Germany countered by using submarines to sink ships headed to British ports. By 1917 German U-boats had destroyed thirty percent of the world's merchant ships.

> "As the liner tilted sharply downwards, the fantail soared a hundred feet in the air, exposing four nearly motionless propellers . . . . She stopped there, frozen still. A long, lingering moan arose and lasted many moments, as though the waters were waiting in horror."

American survivors A. A. Hoehling and Mary Hoehling, describing the May 7, 1915, sinking of the *Lusitania*.

British DeHavilland DH2 airplane (replica by Glenn Huff).

No other dimension of World War I saw such rapid technological advances as air combat. Both sides first used planes for reconnaissance, then began arming them. Pilots fired at each other, dropped bombs, and strafed the trenches. Inventors experimented with two or three wings, swiveling mounts for a second machine gunner, and radio-telegraph communication.

> "I hope he roasted the whole way down."

"Mick" Mannock, top British fighter ace, on hearing of Baron Manfred von Richtofen's death in 1918. Mannock is killed later that year.

Portrait of Woodrow Wilson (1856-1924) by F. Graham Cootes. Wilson won election as U.S. president in 1912, then again in 1916 in the midst of the World War. The artist first met Wilson in 1901.

YEAR OF DECISION

After two and a half years of fighting, Russia had become the weakest member of the Allies. Its battlefield successes were undermined by lack of munitions and supplies, as well as revolution at home. The Germans had managed to stop the Allies on the Italian Front, the Balkan Front, and the Eastern Front. Now, in an attempt to prevail against Britain and France, they decided to renew unrestricted submarine warfare. Before 1917 the United States had never participated in European politics, and it had never fought a major war outside North America. Many Americans believed their country had no reason to fight in this conflict. President Woodrow Wilson had just won re-election with the slogan, "He kept us out of war," and the hit popular song was "I Didn't Raise My Boy to Be a Soldier." In the early months of 1917, however, German policies became more provocative. Sensational headlines reported each new development, raising apprehensions about what future course the U.S. would take.

WHAT AMERICANS WERE READING

American flag that flew over the U.S. Capitol on April 2, 1917, the day President Wilson asked for a declaration of war against Germany.

"The war will thrust America onto the global stage. No matter who wins, can America retreat again into isolationism? The war will transform America's industrial and military might. If the Allies prevail, how will America use its postwar power? There is one certainty—America's horizon has changed."

Patrons viewing film in the Horizon Theater.

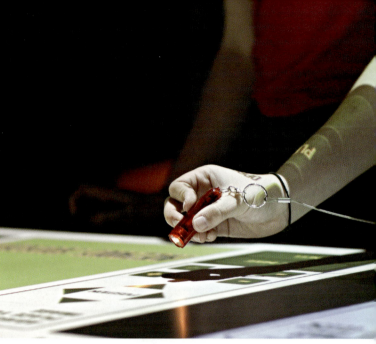

Interactive tables offer visitors the opportunity to take an individual, creative, hands-on approach to learning about topics of WWI history and technology.

1917-1919

On April 6, 1917, President Woodrow Wilson signed the declaration of war against Germany. The United States quickly took steps to put the entire country on a war footing. Millions of men were inducted into the armed forces and given basic combat training. By June 1917 the first U.S. troops were in France. Meantime the Allies suffered serious defeats. In April the disastrous Nivelle Offensive caused widespread mutiny among the French troops. At Passchendaele British casualties surpassed 300,000 during months of fighting in the mud. At Caporetto German and Austrian troops nearly destroyed the Italian army, capturing 250,000 prisoners. By the end of the year Russia was out of the war, which let Germany strengthen its positions in France by transferring thousands of its troops from the Eastern Front. On the sea German U-boats were sinking Allied shipping in record numbers.

Earlier doubts about entering the conflict gave way to an outpouring of enthusiastic support, and within months the war effort transformed the nation. From cities to small towns, Americans rationed food, bought war bonds, worked longer hours, and enlisted in the armed forces. Industries switched to producing munitions, uniforms, and weapons.

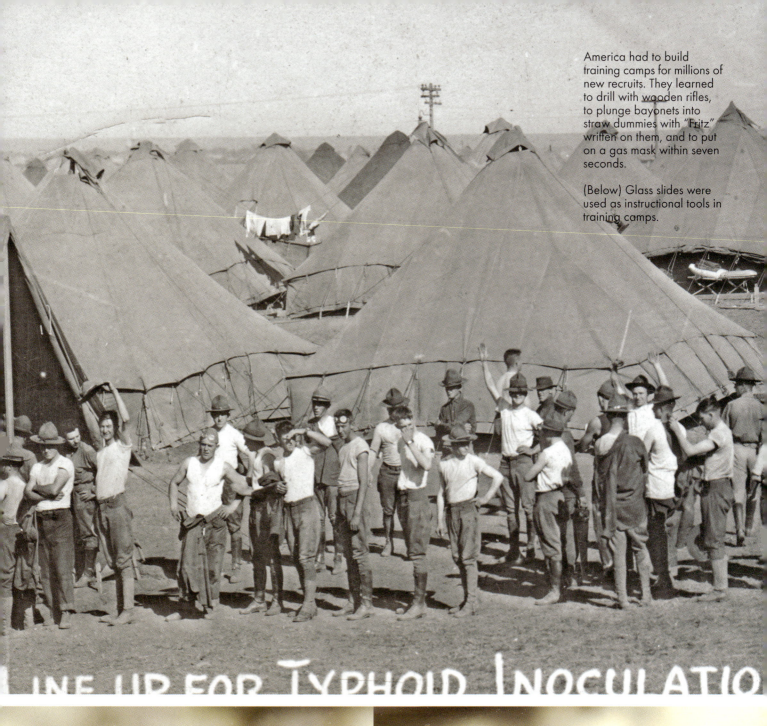

America had to build training camps for millions of new recruits. They learned to drill with wooden rifles, to plunge bayonets into straw dummies with "Fritz" written on them, and to put on a gas mask within seven seconds.

(Below) Glass slides were used as instructional tools in training camps.

LINE UP FOR TYPHOID INOCULATION

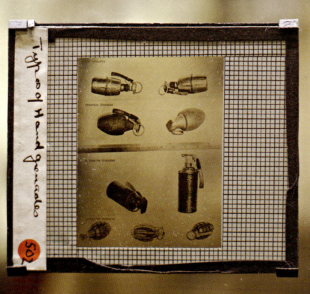

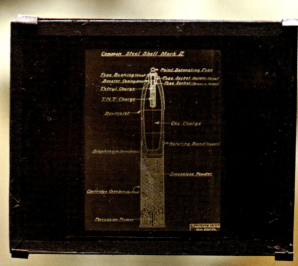

Identity badges worn by workers at a Woodbury, New Jersey, naval ammunition bag loading plant.

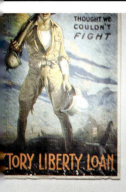

POSTERS & PRINTS

Posters and prints, the sound bites of their day, found their persuasive voice during World War I. After the United States entered the war, "posters literally deluged the country," said one observer. "On every city street, along the rural highways, the posters were to be found repeating their insistent messages day and night." In 1917 James Montgomery Flagg painted a self-portrait as Uncle Sam, creating the most recognizable poster from the war.

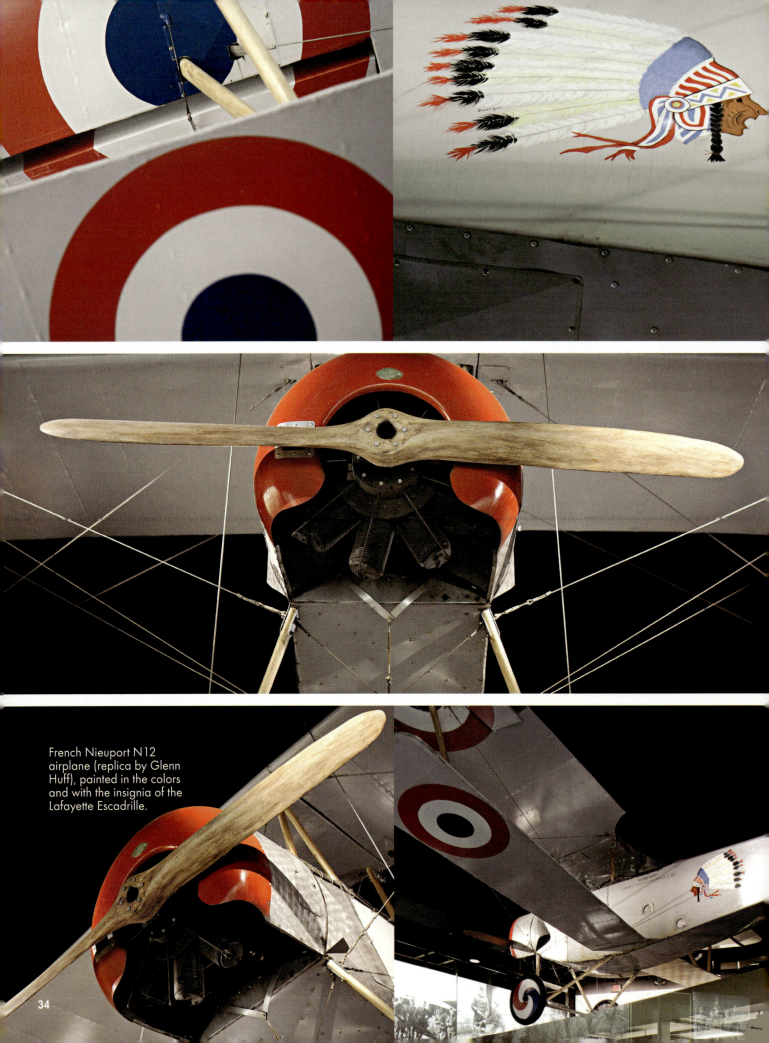

French Nieuport N12 airplane (replica by Glenn Huff), painted in the colors and with the insignia of the Lafayette Escadrille.

When the United States entered the war, its army was small and poorly equipped. Within a year of declaring war, America had assembled an "army of democracy" of nearly four million men and women. The American Expeditionary Forces (AEF) combined units from the regular army, Marines, various state National Guards nationalized by the federal government, and the new National Army created from volunteers and draftees.

SOLDIERS FROM EACH STATE AND TERRITORY

State	Soldiers		State	Soldiers
New York	367,864		Nebraska	47,805
Pennsylvania	297,891		Maryland	47,054
Illinois	251,074		Washington	45,154
Ohio	200,293		Montana	36,293
Texas	161,065		Colorado	34,393
Michigan	135,485		Florida	33,331
Massachusetts	132,610		Oregon	30,116
Missouri	128,544		South Dakota	29,686
California	112,514		North Dakota	25,803
Indiana	106,581		Maine	24,252
New Jersey	105,207		Idaho	19,016
Minnesota	99,116		Utah	17,361
Iowa	98,781		Rhode Island	16,861
Wisconsin	98,211		Puerto Rico	16,538
Georgia	85,506		District of Columbia	15,930
Oklahoma	80,169		New Hampshire	14,374
Tennessee	75,825		New Mexico	12,439
Kentucky	75,043		Wyoming	11,393
Alabama	74,678		Arizona	10,492
Virginia	73,062		Vermont	9,338
North Carolina	73,003		Delaware	7,484
Louisiana	65,988		Hawaii	5,644
Kansas	63,428		Nevada	5,105
Arkansas	61,027		Alaska	2,102
West Virginia	55,777		A.E.F.	1,499
Mississippi	54,295		Not allocated	1,318
South Carolina	53,482		Philippines	255
Connecticut	50,059			

Company I, 139th Infantry, 35th Division, passing through Jarmeuil, France, June 25, 1918.

Eddie Rickenbacker (center), member of the 94th Aero "Hat in the Ring" Squadron and America's leading air ace.

American sailor Ike Skelton III.
Courtesy U.S. Congressman
(D-MO) Ike Skelton IV.

" We are nurses, Red Cross workers, doctors, dentists, civilian employees, ambulance drivers, and mechanics. Women of all sorts and kinds. And we know this thing called war...."

Helen Douglas, ambulance driver, 1917

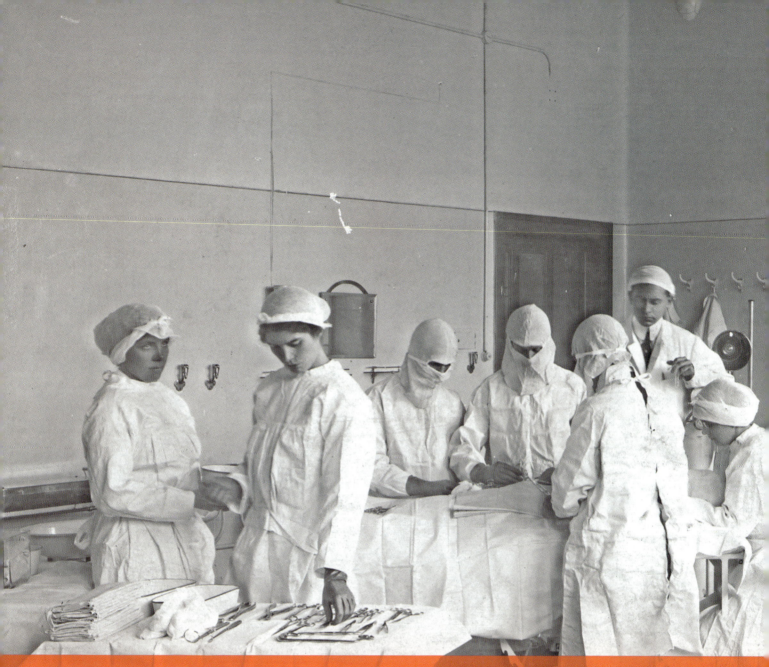

WOMEN IN WAR

About 25,000 women served overseas. They worked as doctors, nurses, drivers, secretaries, and in other important roles that were vital to operations on the Western Front. During the Meuse-Argonne Offensive in the fall 1918, U.S. Signal Corps telephone operators—the "Hello Girls"—transmitted messages from the battlefields to the headquarters of American units. The women worked so close to the front that they kept their gas masks and helmets on the backs of their chairs.

"You can't imagine a more extraordinary mixture Did I tell you the story of the man … who was in the port as a German prisoner of war?"

French observer of U.S. troops, 1918.

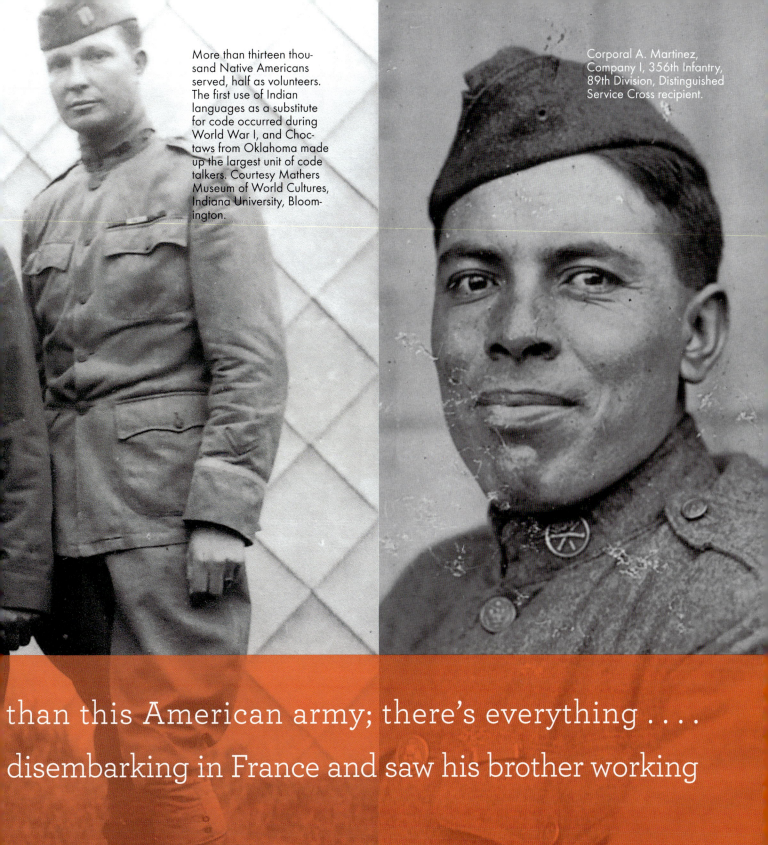

More than thirteen thousand Native Americans served, half as volunteers. The first use of Indian languages as a substitute for code occurred during World War I, and Choctaws from Oklahoma made up the largest unit of code talkers. Courtesy Mathers Museum of World Cultures, Indiana University, Bloomington.

Corporal A. Martinez, Company I, 356th Infantry, 89th Division, Distinguished Service Cross recipient.

than this American army; there's everything . . . . disembarking in France and saw his brother working

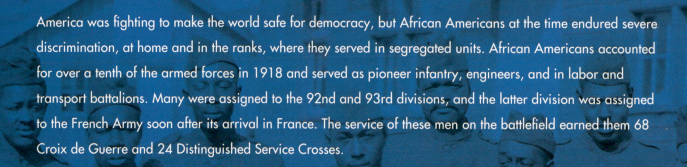

America was fighting to make the world safe for democracy, but African Americans at the time endured severe discrimination, at home and in the ranks, where they served in segregated units. African Americans accounted for over a tenth of the armed forces in 1918 and served as pioneer infantry, engineers, and in labor and transport battalions. Many were assigned to the 92nd and 93rd divisions, and the latter division was assigned to the French Army soon after its arrival in France. The service of these men on the battlefield earned them 68 Croix de Guerre and 24 Distinguished Service Crosses.

> "American blacks in stevedore service were the first American arrivals in France in June 1917. They had been outfitted with [post-Civil-War] over coats: blue with gold buttons and a lining of crimson."
>
> Heywood Broun, correspondent with the American Expeditionary Forces, June 1917.

Corporal Vernon Coffey and Private Virgil McNeal at Orley, France, November 1918.

(Below right) One of the most celebrated units in the war was the 369th Infantry Regiment, 93rd Division (provisional). Their insignia of a rattlesnake inspired their unit's name—the "Black Rattlers."

1918: THE BEGINNING OF THE END

During the spring and early summer of 1918 the Germans pressed their offensives towards Paris and the English Channel. With reinforcements from the Eastern Front they now outnumbered the Allies. Their spring offensive, called "Operation Michael," breached the Allied lines and brought them to the Marne River, the closest the Germans had been to Paris since 1914. At the same time hundreds of thousands of fresh American troops were arriving in France.

The arrival of confident and well-equipped U.S. troops on the Western Front turned the tide of war to the Allies' favor. In March 1918, Germany launched a last, desperate attempt to achieve victory before the American Expeditionary Forces (AEF) could be deployed. But by early 1918, hundreds of thousands of American soldiers were already arriving in France, and more were on the way. The early arrivals fought alongside French divisions at Chateau-Thierry and Belleau Wood. By September the AEF was two million strong and, as a separate army under command of Major General John J. Pershing, ready to begin the Meuse-Argonne Offensive, the last great campaign of the war.

(Above middle) German dog messenger collar. This most modern of wars saw a series of new communication inventions available to the warriors; nevertheless, soldiers on both sides often turned to dogs to send messages on the battlefield. The bell alerted humans not to "shoot the messenger."

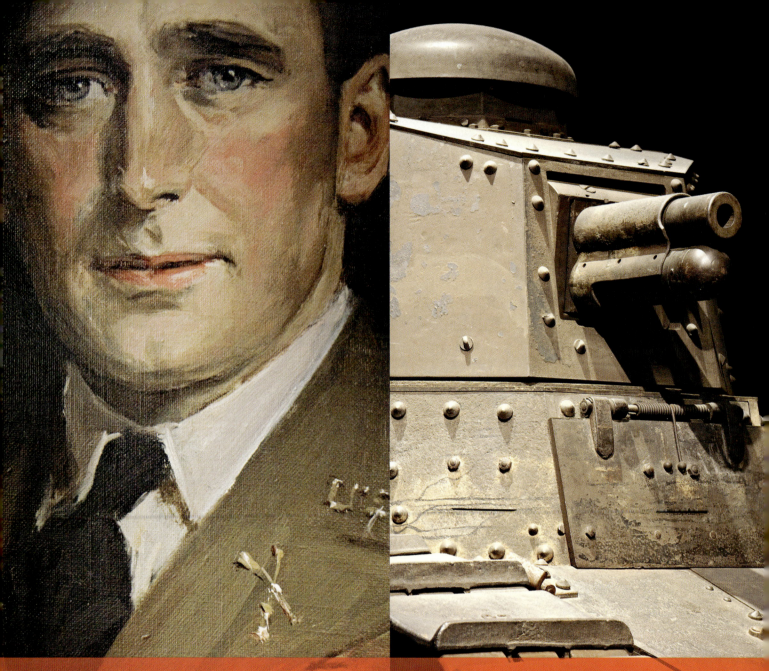

JOHN LEWIS BARKLEY

John Lewis Barkley was a farmer from Johnson County, Missouri, trained at Camp Funston, Kansas, and sent to the front. But what he did one day in October 1918 earned him the Medal of Honor. Barkley held off two German counterattacks with a captured machine gun. According to his citation, he mounted the gun in a disabled French tank, "waited under the hostile barrage until the enemy line was abreast of him and then opened fire, completely breaking up the counterattack and killing or wounding a large number of the enemy. Five minutes later an enemy 77 millimeter gun opened fire on the tank point blank. One shell struck the driver wheel of the tank, but this soldier nevertheless remained in the tank and after the barrage ceased broke up a second counterattack."

By war's end 3,177 Renault tanks were delivered to the French army, 514 to the American Expeditionary Forces, and three to the Italian army. The tank is displayed near General John J. Pershing's four-star, headquarters flag.

BATTLE-SCARRED TANK

During the fighting in the fall 1918 a German 77 mm artillery shell struck this tank in its left rear and put it out of service. The disabled tank found its way to the U.S. 2nd Motor Maintenance Regiment, 2nd Battalion, Air Service Mechanics, who were repairing and salvaging tanks instead of airplanes. During the 1918 Meuse-Argonne Offensive a company of that unit had been sent to Varennes, France, to an improvised tank park. Members of the unit scratched their names on the inside of the driver's compartment armored doors, including Jonathan M. Ashwell, who coincidentally lived in Kansas City, Missouri.

Harley-Davidson 1917 motorcycle, Model J. The museum's example, never restored, retains its original parts and painted surfaces.

Company A, 353rd Infantry Regiment, 89th Division, celebrates the Armistice in Stenay, France.

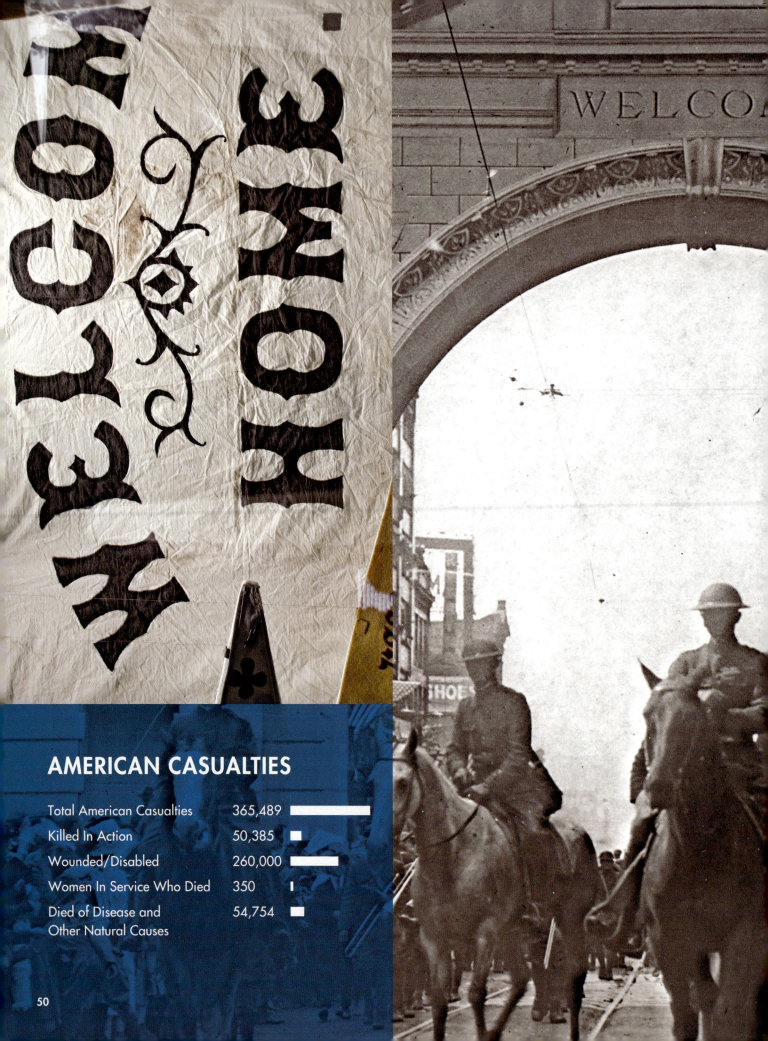

AMERICAN CASUALTIES

Total American Casualties	365,489	
Killed In Action	50,385	
Wounded/Disabled	260,000	
Women In Service Who Died	350	
Died of Disease and Other Natural Causes	54,754	

The American Expeditionary Forces returned to the U.S. over a period of months. Cities and towns across the nation organized huge parades to greet and honor their own. Kansas Citians built a triumphal arch over Grand Avenue.

" Well, this war... is over and the good Lord has been very good to me.... What a relief now to be able to walk down a road without being on edge and ready to drop in a hole at the whistle of a shell."

First Lieutenant James K. Burnham, 354th Infantry, 89th Division, American Expeditionary Forces.

1919: MAKING PEACE

In January a peace conference convened in Paris. The major world leaders—U.S. President Woodrow Wilson, British Prime Minister David Lloyd George, and French Premier Georges Clemenceau—presided over the drafting of the Treaty of Versailles, which would end the war. The Germans were not allowed to negotiate the terms of peace. In June they signed the treaty but protested its harsh conditions. Wilson's primary concern was the League of Nations, and he hoped that it would be able to resolve these issues as well as future conflicts. Congress voted to reject both the Treaty of Versailles and the League of Nations. Later the United States signed its own separate treaty with Germany. It never joined the League.

The United States emerged from the war as a world power, with New York (1931) and its towering skyscrapers as its financial center. Although more war would follow, the hope to end all wars would never die.

"You can't say civilization don't advance, however, for in every war they kill you in a new way."

Will Rogers, American humorist, 1929

RESEARCH & RECHARGE

The Research Center welcomes all those interested in learning more about World War I from the Museum's 55,000 archival and three-dimensional objects and 6,000 library titles. The expansive Research Center is the Museum's resource library of primary and secondary texts, periodicals, and scholarly journals. There is no charge to use the facility, which is located on the lower level of the Museum. From its public research room you can see a ground-level view of the field of poppies. With its delicious food and distinctive ambiance, the *Over There* Café is an exciting addition to the Museum experience. Drawing inspiration for its menu items from the people and places of the Great War, the café's décor includes flags representing participant countries, a poppy mural, and glass etchings of sheet music from the era. Those songs and others can be heard throughout the dining area.

THE LIBERTY MEMORIAL OPENED IN 1926, DEDICATED TO HONOR ALL WHO HAD SERVED IN THE "DEFENSE OF LIBERTY AND OUR COUNTRY" A CROWD OF OVER ONE HUNDRED THOUSAND, MANY OF THEM AMERICAN VETERANS, PARTICIPATED IN THE NOVEMBER 11 CEREMONY, WITH PRESIDENT CALVIN COOLIDGE PRESIDING.

Over eight decades later, the view of the Liberty Memorial has changed relatively little. Although your grandparents would recognize the memorial, they would scarcely conceive the modern, twenty-first-century museum that now resides under its deck. Carved from the space under the original memorial, the resultant masterpiece received the prestigious Institute Honor Award for Architecture from the American Institute of Architects.

In 2004 the Liberty Memorial received from the U.S. Department of Interior the coveted designation of National Historic Landmark, recognition of its great historical and architectural significance. The original planners of the memorial had wisely placed the imposing structure on a hill above Union Station, the twentieth-century, central gateway to Kansas City.

Sculptures of guardian spirits, representing courage, honor, patriotism, and sacrifice sit atop the tower. This view (below center) came from the original architectural plans.

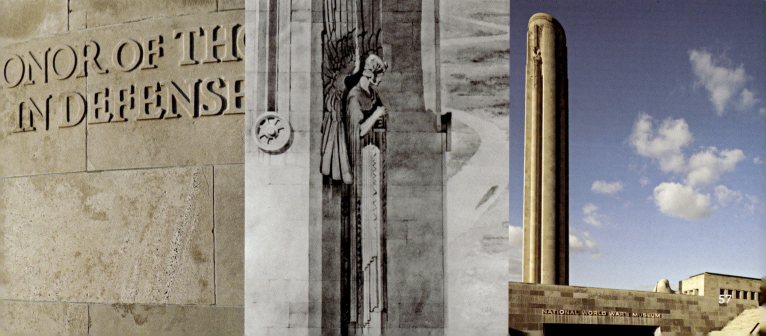

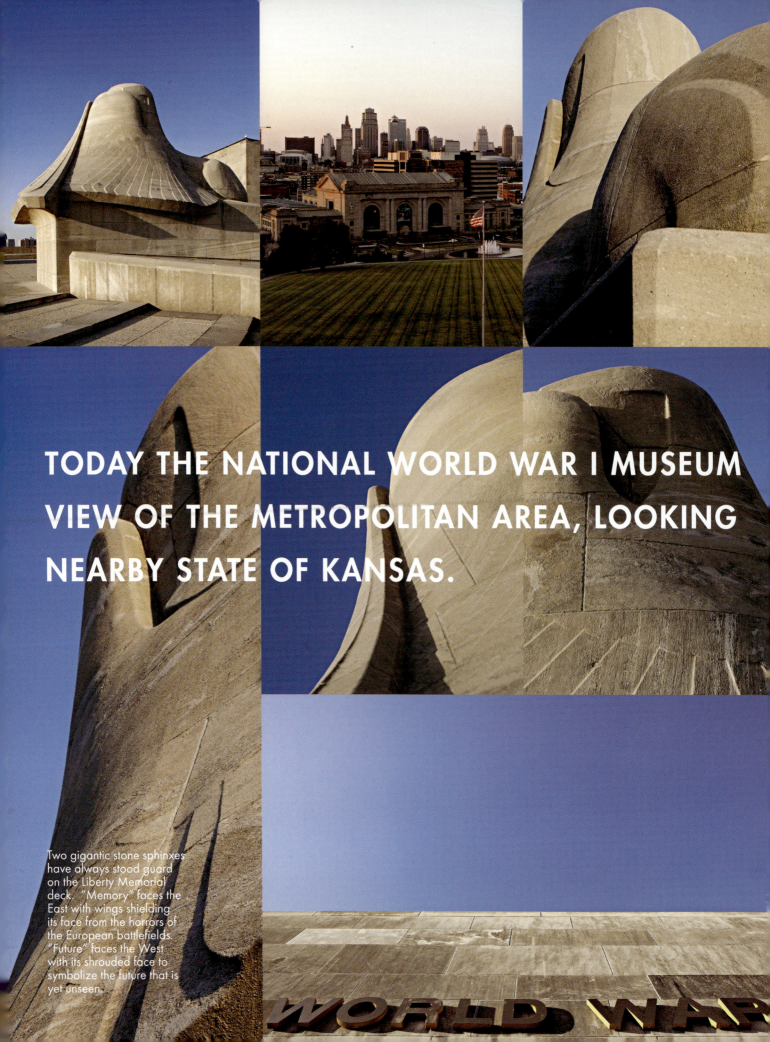

TODAY THE NATIONAL WORLD WAR I MUSEUM VIEW OF THE METROPOLITAN AREA, LOOKING NEARBY STATE OF KANSAS.

Two gigantic stone sphinxes have always stood guard on the Liberty Memorial deck. "Memory" faces the East with wings shielding its face from the horrors of the European battlefields. "Future" faces the West with its shrouded face to symbolize the future that is yet unseen.

AT LIBERTY MEMORIAL STILL ENJOYS A SWEEPING WEST FROM KANSAS CITY, MISSOURI TO THE

After the 1926 opening a few architectural features remained to be completed, including the Great Frieze on the north wall. Sculpted by Edmond Amateis in 1934-35, the artwork depicts civilization's progress from war to peace. It remains one of the world's largest such stone carvings, measuring 148 feet long and eighteen feet tall.

Each of the nine thousand poppies on display represents a thousand combatant deaths, a total of nine million dead.